COMPLETE

BEE FARMING

PRO GUIDE

A Comprehensive Guide To Sustainable Beekeeping, Honey Production, Pollination Techniques, And Hive Management For Beginners And Experts

VERN WILSON

Chapter 1
Introducing Bee Farming

Growing bees for their honey, beeswax, and other products including royal jelly and propolis is known as bee farming, or apiculture. This age-old craft has been carried out for millennia since the Greeks and Egyptians were among the first civilizations to value bees for their honey and saw them as fertility and plenty of emblems. In agriculture and the environment today, beekeeping is essential, greatly enhancing biodiversity and pollination. Explored in detail in this thorough book are the significance, advantages, and possible markets for bee products.

Value of Beekeeping

The value of beekeeping goes much beyond the yield of honey. Essential pollinators, bees are vital to the reproduction of blooming plants, including many food crops. About 75% of the world's food crops rely, at least partially, on pollination by bees and other pollinators, according to the Food and Agriculture Organization (FAO) of the UN.

This dependence on pollinators emphasizes how important beekeeping is to both agricultural sustainability and world food security.

In addition, by encouraging biodiversity, beekeeping helps to preserve the ecosystem. Pollinating wild plants as well as crops, bees assist wildlife and improve the health of ecosystems. For many species, including insects, birds, and mammals, floral variety is vital, and their efforts assist in preserving it. Thus, beekeeping supports ecological stewardship and sustainable agriculture, thus improving the environment for current and future generations.

Aspects of Bee Farming

Bee farming offers many advantages that include areas of nutrition, ecology, and economy. Economically speaking, selling honey, beeswax, bee pollen, royal jelly, propolis, and even bee colonies provides beekeepers with a source of revenue. Because honey in particular is such a valuable commodity with so many applications in food, medicine, and cosmetics, beekeeping is a lucrative endeavor for many farmers and businesspeople.

Environmentally, by improving pollination services, bee farming promotes biodiversity and ecosystem resilience. Fruits, vegetables, nuts, and oilseeds are just a few of the plant species that bees help reproduce, which increases agricultural productivity and genetic variety. Additionally, conservation and sustainable land management are promoted by beekeeping techniques including preserving bee-friendly habitats and avoiding dangerous chemicals.

Consumers of bee products gain nutritionally. One natural sweetener with antioxidant and antibacterial qualities is honey. Its wound-healing qualities and use as a cough and sore throat treatment are well known in traditional medicine. The possible health-promoting qualities of other bee products, such as propolis and royal jelly, are also highly appreciated; these include skin care and immune support.

The need for natural, sustainable, and premium goods by consumers is driving the broad and growing market potential for bee products. A mainstay of the beekeeping business, honey is still produced in a variety of floral sources, flavors, and processing techniques to suit a wide range of customer tastes. Because of their special qualities and supposed health advantages, specialty honey—like New Zealand manuka honey and European acacia honey—command higher prices.

Another priceless ingredient with many uses in candles, cosmetics, medications, and handicrafts is beeswax. Because of its emollient and natural waterproofing qualities, it is a highly sought-after component in ointments, lip balms, and skincare products. High in proteins, vitamins, and minerals, bee pollen is promoted as a dietary supplement with supposed health advantages including allergy treatment and immune support.

Prized for its nutritional content and possible health-promoting properties, royal jelly is a fluid made by worker bees to feed larvae and queen bees.

Many times, it is sold as a dietary supplement or component of cosmetics, with claims of better energy, hormonal balance, and skin health. Because it is antibacterial and anti-inflammatory, propolis—a resinous material bees gather from tree buds—is a useful component of natural cures and dental care products.

The natural origin, nutritional worth, and ecological significance of bee products are driving the market's ongoing expansion worldwide. Health-conscious customers go for items made of honey, bee pollen, royal jelly, propolis, and beeswax because of their sustainable manufacturing techniques and claimed health benefits. A further factor driving interest in beekeeping and the growth of niche markets for high-end bee products is the trend toward organic and environmentally friendly goods.

Finally, beekeeping is essential to economic growth, environment, and agriculture. Its value as a pollination service provider, manufacturer of worthwhile goods, and advocate of biodiversity emphasizes the need to endorse sustainable beekeeping methods. The market for bee goods is set for further expansion and innovation as customers value natural and sustainable products more and more. This presents chances for beekeepers, entrepreneurs, and environmentally concerned consumers.

Chapter 2

Getting Started

Beginning beekeeping requires an understanding of a few fundamental ideas that are essential to the success of this project. Selecting the proper bee species for your bee farm is one of your first choices. The location, climate, and reason for beekeeping—whether it be for pollination services, honey production, or both—all affect the species of bees you choose.

Because native bee species are frequently well-suited to the local habitat and climate, take them into account when choosing a species. Several local bee species, such as bumblebees and solitary bees, are efficient pollinators, as is the European honeybee (Apis mellifera), which is extensively employed for honey production.

Several stages go into establishing a bee farm so that bees may live, make honey, or help with pollination. Because bees need to be able to reach food sources like nectar and pollen, location is very important to beekeeping. Select a spot where there are a variety of flowering plants that can offer nourishment all year long.

Minimizing pesticide use and offering bees sources of water to drink are other aspects of creating a bee-friendly environment. For bees to visit your farm, think about planting lavender, sunflowers, and wildflowers.

For beekeeping to be safe for both the beekeeper and the bees, equipment is vital. Basic beekeeping supplies include gloves, veils, and bee jackets to keep one safe from bee stings. While manipulating hive components, bees are calmed using a smoker during hive inspections.

A key piece of beekeeping equipment is the hive itself. Two popular hive kinds are top-bar hives, which contain bars in place of frames and are frequently used in natural beekeeping techniques, and Langstroth hives, which are stacked boxes with detachable frames for honey extraction and hive management.

Bee brushes are other tools required for beekeeping, as are feeders for giving bees more food during dry spells and extractors and filters for extracting honey.

All things considered, learning which bee species are best for your farm, creating a bee-friendly environment, and collecting the tools you need to properly manage and care for bee hives are all part of beginning beekeeping. A fulfilling and long-lasting agricultural activity, beekeeping can be done with the right information and planning.

Chapter 3
Bee Biology And Behavior

Appreciating Bee Anatomy

A fascinating field, bee anatomy explores the complex structures and functions of these essential pollinators. Members of the order Hymenoptera, bees have developed over millions of years into highly specialized insects with distinct adaptations for their function in pollination and honey production.

The segmented body of bees, which consists of three primary sections—the head, thorax, and abdomen—is among their most characteristic characteristics. Important sensory organs, notably the compound eyes, which allow bees to see ultraviolet light and precisely navigate their environment, are housed in the head. Furthermore, bees need their antennae to detect chemicals and pheromones, which are necessary for both communication inside the hive and foraging outside.

Turning now to the thorax, bees have six legs with specific adaptations for gathering pollen and launching themselves into flight. Bees' hind legs are converted into corbiculae, or pollen baskets, where they keep pollen grains collected from flowers. Both plant pollination and the nourishment of the bee colony depend on this pollen.

Important systems like the digestive system, reproductive organs, and sting mechanisms are found in bees' abdomen. A modified ovipositor, the sting of a bee is employed mostly for defense but is also used during mating. But only female bees have stings; males, dubbed drones, do not have this protection mechanism.

Timeline of Bees

Conservationists as well as beekeepers must understand the life cycle of bees. Bees go through all the developmental stages—egg, larva, pupa, and adult—and completely change.

In the comb of the hive, the queen bee first deposits her eggs.

Unfertilized eggs become male drones; fertilized eggs grow into female worker bees or possible future queens. Workers feed the larvae a nutrient-dense material called royal jelly after they hatch from the eggs. Potential queens are encouraged to develop by this royal jelly; these queens will then continue to eat and grow in specialized queen cells.

Most of the colony are worker bees, who as they get older move through a variety of jobs. Beginning with nursing responsibilities, they tend to the brood and keep the hive tidy. As they get older, they take on new responsibilities like beeswax production, hive protection, nectar, pollen, and water seeking.

Conversely, drones exist in the colony just to mate with a virgin queen from another colony. They never help to maintain the hive or forage, and when resources are scarce or winter draws near, they are eventually driven out.

Larvae become fully formed adult bees during the pupal stage. At this point, as the bee's organs and systems fully develop, there are major physiological changes.

After emerging from its pupal cell, an adult bee either starts working inside the hive or goes out to forage, carrying on the cycle of colony development and output.

Bee in the Hive Behavior

Within the hive, bees engage in intricate social activities propelled by a well-structured caste system and effective division of work. The queen, workers, and drones—all with particular duties and responsibilities—live in the hive.

The queen bee is the primary character in the hive; she lays the eggs and keeps the colony reproducing. Her pheromones control hive harmony and behavior, impacting everything from swarm behavior to worker bee activity.

Most of the colony are worker bees, who do a wide range of jobs necessary for the survival of the hive.

Among these include feeding larvae, constructing and maintaining the hive, searching for food, watching over the entrance, and controlling hive temperature by fanning or clustering. Through the complex waggle dance, worker bees communicate direction and distance from food sources.

Less in number, drones are essential to the reproductive activity of the hive. Their only goal is to mate with virgin queens from neighboring colonies, therefore enhancing genetic variety in the bee population. Working bees provide the drones with their food; they do not go foraging or maintain hives.

Seasonal variations, resource availability, and the weather all have an impact on bee activity inside the hive as well. Bees swarm to form new colonies, cluster in cold weather, and distribute resources according to the availability of nectar and pollen as adaptive behaviors to maximize hive operation and survival.

All things considered, the complex biology and behavior of bees emphasize how vitally important they are to ecosystems as pollinators and makers of honey.

Knowledge of these features not only enhances our understanding of these amazing insects but also guides sustainable beekeeping methods and conservation initiatives to ensure their ongoing health and contribution to biodiversity.

Chapter 4
<u>Of The Hive</u>

Many techniques are included in hive management that are essential to the proper maintenance of bee colonies. Deep knowledge of bee behavior, hive dynamics, and environmental variables affecting bee health and productivity is required. Fundamental to good hive management are methods for swarm prevention and control, hive health maintenance, and inspection techniques.

Understanding the condition of a bee colony and taking quick care of any problems need knowledge of hive inspection techniques. Regular inspections let beekeepers keep an eye on the general condition of the hive, determine the number of bees, look for diseases or pests, calculate the amount of honey produced, and make sure all the hive's parts are operating as they should. Beekeepers use a variety of techniques when inspecting, including eye observation, employing smokers to quiet bees, and closely inspecting frames for cleanliness, honey reserves, and brood patterns.

These methods enable beekeepers to decide with knowledge whether to add or remove frames, treat illnesses or pests, or give extra nutrition as needed as part of hive management procedures.

A vital component of beekeeping is hive health maintenance, which is taking preventative steps to ward against diseases, pests, and other stresses that might harm bee colonies. This covers making sure the hive is ventilated properly, has enough forage supplies, and has access to clean water. To reduce the number of chemical treatments that can damage bees and taint hive products, beekeepers also use integrated pest management (IPM) techniques to control pests including wax moths, hive beetles, and Varroa mites. Hive health and production are improved overall by routine maintenance chores including cleaning equipment, changing old combs, and looking for symptoms of stress or illness.

It takes swarm prevention and management for beekeepers to keep hive populations stable and stop bees from swarming out.

Although honeybee colonies naturally swarm for reproduction, overdoing it can weaken hives and lower honey output. Beekeepers manage colony congestion, give enough space inside the hive, and make sure the queen has enough place to lay eggs as ways to stop swarming. Swarming tendencies can be lessened and overpopulation lessened with methods including checkerboarding frames, supers, and colony splitting. Furthermore, to catch swarms and keep them from leaving the apiary, beekeepers may utilize bait hives or swarm traps, therefore protecting important bee populations.

All things considered, good hive management calls for a blend of expertise, abilities, and preventative steps to guarantee the longevity, productivity, and health of bee colonies. Through the development of hive inspection skills, hive health maintenance, and swarm prevention and management plans, beekeepers may promote healthy bee populations and enhance the health of pollinator ecosystems.

Chapter 5
Bee Nutrition And Feeds

Conservationists as well as beekeepers must understand bee nutrition and feeding. Because they are so important to pollination and ecosystem health, bees—especially honeybees—must have enough food to remain healthy and productive. This talk explores bee nutritional requirements, efficient feeding techniques, and additional feeding alternatives to promote bee health.

For their general health and growth, bees have particular nutritional needs. Carbs, proteins, lipids, vitamins, minerals, and water make up their diet. The main sources of carbohydrates for bee activities including foraging, hive care, and thermoregulation are nectar and honey. From the pollen that forager bees gather, proteins are necessary for both larval growth and adult tissue repair. While vitamins and minerals support many physiological activities, fats and oils help to build cell membranes and produce hormones.

The principal sources of proteins and carbohydrates, respectively, are pollen and nectar that foraging bees gather from flowers. Because it is high in carbohydrates like fructose and glucose, nectar gives bees quick energy and is used as the raw material to make honey. Conversely, pollen is an important supply of protein with the amino acids required for bee development and reproduction. Furthermore gathering resin and water for hive building and upkeep are bees.

Especially in places with little floral resources or during particular seasons, beekeepers are essential in making sure bees have enough food. Bee numbers are monitored, local flora are understood, and extra nourishment is provided as needed as part of feeding plans for bee health. When natural nectar becomes scarce or to promote hive expansion, beekeepers frequently replace it with sugar syrup. The amount of sugar in the syrup and any additions, such as essential oils or pollen substitutes, can affect the health and output of the bees.

Bees have other dietary choices, such as protein supplements and pollen substitutes, to supplement their natural pollen supplies. Natural pollen is reproduced nutritionally in pollen substitutes, which supply vital vitamins and amino acids needed for bee growth. Additionally improving bee nutrition are protein additives like soybean or pea flour, particularly in times of low pollen or unfavorable foraging conditions. But to guarantee these supplements satisfy bees' nutritional needs without causing any problems, much attention must be paid to their quality and composition.

Bees need micronutrients like vitamins and minerals for best health in addition to proteins and carbs. While these micronutrients are naturally present in pollen, in inadequate conditions additional feeding may be required. To guarantee bees get the minerals they need for physiological processes like enzyme activity and immune system support, beekeepers can use mineral supplements like salt or mineral blocks. Commercial vitamins and natural sources like bee bread—a fermented concoction of pollen, honey, and secretions—can both supply vitamins.

A further vital part of bee nutrition, water is utilized for honey diluting, brood raising, and hive cooling. Near hives, beekeepers frequently place water supplies, including shallow trays with floating items for bees to land on while drinking. It takes clean, easily available water to keep bees from becoming dehydrated and to keep them busy.

All things considered, sustaining pollination services necessary for agriculture and ecological balance and preserving healthy bee populations depend critically on an understanding of bee nutrition and feeding. Beekeepers may support the health and resilience of their bees in a variety of environmental conditions by giving them enough water, carbohydrates, proteins, vitamins, and minerals from natural sources and additional feeding alternatives. Sustainable beekeeping and conservation efforts depend heavily on routine monitoring, appropriate hive management, and attention to nutritional demands.

Chapter 6
Bees And Harvesting

The intriguing realm of natural resources that bee products and harvesting cover has been used by people for ages. The four primary bee product categories—honey, beeswax, propolis, and pollen—are all valuable in traditional medicine and agriculture in addition to the culinary and cosmetic industries because of their individual qualities and uses. Consumers and beekeepers alike must be aware of the nuances of processing procedures, harvesting tactics, and packaging issues.

Of all the bee products, honey is the most well-known and eaten. The sweet flavor and variety of tastes—from fruity to floral—depend on the nectar sources that bees acquire. When bees have stored honey in wax cells in beehives, beekeepers carefully remove frames from the hives. The wax caps must be removed, the frames must be spun in a centrifuge to release the honey, and any contaminants must be filtered out. Because of its special flavor characteristics and health benefits, raw honey—which is barely processed and retains its natural enzymes and nutrients—is much sought for.

A further useful bee product is beeswax, which bees make to construct their honeycomb cells. Beekeepers may get beeswax by delicately scraping it off the frames or by removing it from the comb using specialized equipment. Famous for its adaptability, beeswax finds usage in cosmetics, skincare items, candle making, and even as a food-grade coating for cheeses and fruits. To keep beeswax pure and of high quality, it must be harvested carefully.

One resinous material bees get from tree buds and sap flows is called propolis, sometimes called "bee glue." Propolis is used to fill up gaps in the hive and keep germs out. Propolis is harvested by either utilizing traps that encourage bees to deposit propolis in certain locations or by scraping it off hive surfaces. Because of its antioxidant and antibacterial qualities, this natural substance has become well-known and is a useful component of natural treatments, cosmetics products, and health supplements.

Less well recognized than honey or beeswax, pollen is essential to bee nutrition and the health of the environment. Bee bread is made when bees combine pollen from flowers with nectar to provide their larvae with protein. Specialized traps that gather pollen pellets when bees enter the hive allow beekeepers to capture pollen. Being high in vitamins, minerals, and amino acids, pollen is a well-liked dietary supplement and component of nutritional goods.

The kind of bee product and the beekeeper's methods determine how to harvest it. For honey, beekeepers must plan their harvests to fall during the highest nectar flows and guarantee appropriate extraction and storage conditions to preserve quality.

The natural qualities of beeswax must be preserved and pollution avoided by cautious handling during harvesting. When harvesting propolis, traps or other collection techniques are placed strategically to reduce disturbance to the hive and bees' work. The goal of pollen harvesting is to gather pellets of pollen without endangering bees or hive health.

The steps to clean, purify, and get bee products ready for use commercially or for human consumption are called processing. Filtration, heating to liquefaction, and jar or container packing are all part of honey processing. For particular textures and consistencies, beekeepers may use cream honey.

Processed beeswax is pure beeswax blocks or pellets prepared for a variety of uses after melting and filtering to eliminate debris and contaminants. Processed propolis may be concentrated into tinctures or extracts by solvent or alcohol extraction. To keep pollen nutritious and prolong shelf life, it is dried and packaged.

Keeping bee products safe, fresh, and of high quality requires careful packaging. Generally speaking, honey is sold in squeeze bottles, plastic containers, or glass jars with labels that detail its processing techniques, source of flowers, and origin. Products made of beeswax come in blocks, sheets, or molded shapes and are kept fresh and texture-preserving by being sealed in airtight receptacles. Many times, propolis tinctures and extracts are packaged in dark glass to keep light from deteriorating them. To keep its nutritious content and stop moisture absorption, pollen is packed in sealed bags or containers.

Ultimately, bee products and harvesting include a wide range of natural resources with many uses and advantages. For beekeepers, consumers, and industries that depend on these priceless gifts from the hive, knowing the kinds of bee products—honey, beeswax, propolis, and pollen—as well as their harvesting, processing, and packaging issues, is crucial. Ecosystem health and bee populations are greatly aided by ethical beekeeping and sustainable methods as long as we value and use bee products.

Chapter 7
Management Of Bee Health And Diseases

Essential to beekeeping are bee health and disease management, which needs in-depth knowledge of prevalent bee diseases, prevention measures, and available treatments. Important for pollination, bees greatly increase biodiversity and agricultural production. But just as any other living thing, bees are vulnerable to several illnesses that can compromise the health and output of their colonies. Maintaining healthy bee populations depends on knowing these diseases, taking preventive actions, and having efficient treatment choices.

Numerous conditions that might affect bee colonies are referred to as common bee diseases. American foulbrood, or AFB, is one of the most common illnesses brought on by the bacteria

Paenibacillus larvae. Mostly, AFB damages honeybee larvae, which die and eventually cause the colony to decline.

European foulbrood, or EFB, is another prevalent illness brought on by the bacteria Melissococcus plutonius. While it can also affect adult bees, EFB also affects larvae and can result in symptoms like discolored larvae and splotchy brood patterns. Because it affects the digestive tract of bees, Nosema disease—caused by the microsporidian parasite Nosema apis or Nosema ceranae—reduces bee lifespan and colony output.

Maintaining bee health and stopping illness outbreaks mostly depend on preventative actions. Beekeepers have several options for lowering the possibility of disease spread inside their colonies.

By routinely cleaning and sanitizing hive equipment, for example, you can stop the accumulation and spread of infections. Bees can also have their immune systems strengthened and their resistance to diseases increased by giving them a varied and nourishing diet with easy access to pollen and nectar sources. Maintaining enough ventilation and room in the hive is one way that good hive management can also assist avoid stress-related problems that increase bee vulnerability to diseases.

Beekeepers can choose from several approaches for treating bee illnesses. If antibiotics are started early in the infection and followed by advised procedures, they can be useful for bacterial disorders such as AFB and EFB. Antibiotic resistance and the effects of these treatments on the environment and bee health are worries, though, thus other strategies like organic acids or biocontrol agents are also being investigated. The fungus Ascosphaera apis causes chalkbrood, one of the fungal diseases that can be controlled by cultural techniques including changing contaminated comb and preserving ideal hive conditions.

Apart from particular remedies for certain diseases, beekeepers can use comprehensive strategies to enhance the general health and disease resistance of their bees. This covers techniques like integrated pest management (IPM), which combines biological, chemical, and cultural control techniques to reduce pest and disease burdens.

For instance, screened bottom boards can help stop Varroa mite infestations, which are carriers of several bee viruses, and hence lessen the spread of disease inside colonies. Moreover, long-term bee health and disease control depends on continuous study into creating sustainable beekeeping techniques and breeding disease-resistant bee stocks.

Finally, while being intricate, bee health and disease control are essential parts of beekeeping. Beekeepers may encourage robust and healthy bee populations by learning about typical bee diseases, putting preventative measures into place, and investigating different treatment possibilities. Achieving present goals and guaranteeing the ongoing health of bees and their essential contributions to ecosystems and agriculture need sustainable beekeeping techniques, continuous research, and cooperation within the beekeeping community.

Chapter 8
Advanced Beekeeping Practices

A variety of techniques and strategies are included in sustainable beekeeping operations to protect the health and welfare of honeybee colonies while reducing adverse effects on the environment.

One of the mainstays of sustainable beekeeping, organic beekeeping stresses non-synthetic, natural techniques for managing hives and producing honey. With this method, using natural hive materials, organic beekeeping supplies like organic sugar for feeding bees when needed, and wooden hives without chemical treatments are given top priority.

The promotion of bee health by natural means is essential to organic beekeeping techniques. Among these is giving bees a varied, pesticide-free habitat so they can browse a range of plants and wildflowers without coming into contact with dangerous toxins.

By choosing and raising bees that exhibit great resistance to diseases and pests, organic beekeepers also aim to improve the natural resilience of bee colonies, therefore lowering the necessity for chemical treatments.

Environmental factors are quite important in sustainable beekeeping methods. Beekeepers cultivate bee-friendly plants, steer clear of bee-harming chemicals, and provide native bee species places to nest to produce bee-friendly landscapes that benefit pollinator populations. Beekeepers support ecosystem health and biodiversity, therefore enhancing the general sustainability of natural habitats and agricultural landscapes.

A major technique in sustainable beekeeping, integrated pest management (IPM) seeks to control disease and pest stresses in bee colonies by a comprehensive and ecologically friendly method. Using biological controls like predatory mites to selectively target pest populations, mechanical controls like screened bottom boards to reduce varroa mite infestations and routine hive health monitoring are all part of integrated pest management.

Beekeepers can lessen their need for chemical treatments and lower their chance of insect populations gaining resistance by combining several pest management strategies.

Furthermore, ethical hive management methods—like not overharvesting honey or overstressing colonies during honey extraction—are stressed in sustainable beekeeping methods. To preserve colony health and stability, beekeepers give their bees enough food, control hive temperature and ventilation, and put swarm avoidance techniques into place.

To share best practices, support research on bee health and genetics, and promote laws that protect pollinators and their habitats, beekeepers also need to educate and engage the public. By participating in continuous education and information exchange, beekeepers support the group's efforts to maintain healthy bee populations for pollination, honey production, and ecosystem resilience.

Chapter 9
Building Your Bee Farm

Scaling up production, diversifying bee products, and successfully promoting and selling these items are just a few of the many important components of expanding a bee farm. Many times, beekeepers who want to boost their yields and satisfy rising demand want to scale up production. Product diversification of bees enables beekeepers to enter new markets and increase their sources of income. Reaching target clients and increasing sales need having effective marketing plans. Let us explore every one of these ideas in more detail.

For beekeepers hoping to grow their business and produce more honey, scaling up production is a calculated step. Starting with assessing the present production capacity and pinpointing areas for development, this process consists of several important stages. Beekeepers could want to think about growing their apiary by getting extra hives or colonies.

For the best possible hive management, enough room, and enough resources—like food and water for the bees—this growth needs meticulous preparation.

In addition to growing their hives, beekeepers may make investments in contemporary equipment and technology to increase productivity.

This covers equipment for controlling insects, extracting honey, and managing hives. Scaling up requires also the use of sustainable beekeeping techniques, which guarantee the long-term health and production of the bee colonies.

Another approach that can be quite advantageous to beekeepers is diversifying their bee products. Although the main output of bee farms is honey, there are many other worthwhile products as well.

These might be bee venom, royal jelly, propolis, pollen, and beeswax. Every one of these substances has special qualities and possible applications in different sectors, such as supplements, medications, and cosmetics.

Successful diversification of bee products requires beekeepers to comprehend market demand, product quality standards, and regulatory restrictions.

They could have to make investments in more facilities and equipment to process and package these goods. Working together with regional companies or craftspeople might also open up chances to produce goods with added value, including skin care items with honey or beeswax candles.

To reach intended consumers and increase sales, bee product marketing and sales need a well-thought-out approach. Local markets, internet sites, and specialized shops are just a few of the venues that beekeepers might use to present their goods. Developing a strong brand identity and emphasizing the special attributes of their bee products can draw in clients and foster a devoted following.

Marketing tactics that work include producing interesting material about beekeeping techniques, holding informative seminars or events, and collaborating with influencers or groups that support sustainable agriculture and bee conservation. Additionally, beekeepers might look for chances to sell their goods abroad to meet the demand for premium bee products worldwide.

To put it briefly, growing a bee farm means increasing output, broadening the range of bee products, and putting good marketing plans into practice. Carefully organizing and carrying out these tactics can help beekeepers fulfill market demand, expand their business, and support the sustainability of beekeeping methods.

Chapter 10
The Advanced Techniques And Technologies

Queen Bee Rearing

A vital component of beekeeping and queen bee rearing is the careful breeding and care of queen bees for the best possible health and production of the hive.

Bee biology, behavior, and genetics must be thoroughly understood for this process.

To properly rear queen bees, beekeepers use a variety of methods and technologies meant to enhance the genetic features and qualities of the queen bees. Artificial insemination is one of the main techniques employed; queen bees are inseminated using semen from chosen drones with desired characteristics. Beekeepers can so regulate the genetic variety and caliber of the queen bee's progeny.

Grafting is a further method of queen bee rearing in which larvae are moved from worker bee cells into specifically designed queen cups.

To guarantee the larvae grow into healthy queen bees, this process calls for accuracy and dexterity. Queen excluders are also used by beekeepers to stop the queen from depositing eggs in honeycomb cells set aside for storing honey, therefore preserving the brood chambers for the rearing of new queens.

Technologies in beekeeping have also resulted in the creation of queen-rearing kits and other tools that make beekeeping easier. Many times, these kits come with queen cups, grafting equipment, and queen cages made to keep and move just mated queen bees.

Further important aspects of queen bee rearing are breeding programs and genetic testing. Superior queen beelines are developed by beekeepers working with scientists and researchers to find and spread genetic features including illness resistance, productivity, and kindness.

Comprehensive projects aiming at increasing the genetic variety, resilience, and productivity of bee populations are known as bee breeding programs. Keeping bee populations healthy and viable requires these initiatives, particularly in the face of obstacles like diseases, pests, and environmental changes.

Choosing and multiplying bee colonies with desired characteristics, like disease resistance, honey production efficiency, gentle temperament, and winter hardiness, is one of the main objectives of bee breeding projects. Bee colonies are carefully evaluated in this procedure using genetic analysis and performance indicators.

Utilizing cutting-edge technology like genomics, modern bee breeding operations can select breeding stock with exact genetic profiling. Breeders of bees can find genes linked to desirable characteristics by genetic testing and include them in breeding plans to improve the general health and productivity of the colony.

Agricultural institutions, researchers, and beekeepers frequently work together on bee breeding programs. Through these alliances, best practices for sustainable beekeeping can be developed, data gathering and knowledge sharing facilitated.

Bee breeding programs concentrate not just on genetic selection but also on enhancing bee management techniques like hive design, pest control techniques, and nutrition supplementing. Bee breeding projects provide a major contribution to the durability and success of beekeeping operations throughout the world by fusing scientific discoveries with technical advancements.

Innovations in Beekeeping Today

A variety of cutting-edge tools and techniques that have transformed the beekeeping sector and enhanced bee health, productivity, and sustainability are what define modern beekeeping. These developments include everything from hive management to honey extraction and hive monitoring in beekeeping.

Among the noteworthy advancements in contemporary beekeeping is the creation of smart hives with sensors and monitoring equipment. Beekeepers may now remotely check hive parameters including temperature, humidity, hive weight, and bee activity using these cutting-edge hives. Beekeepers may decide with knowledge about hive health and management thanks to this real-time data.

Further developments in hive design have produced practical and effective hive parts including queen excluders, ventilation systems, and modular frames. These improvements raise hive productivity generally, lower stress, and improve colony comfort.

Modern beekeeping has witnessed the development of integrated pest management (IPM) tactics that blend chemical, biological, and cultural control techniques for pest and disease management. While successfully controlling illnesses and pests that might damage bee colonies, IPM techniques give priority to environmentally benign methods.

In addition, filtering systems, uncapping machines, and automated honey extractors have all greatly advanced honey extraction technology. Through the simplification of the honey harvesting procedure, labor expenses are decreased and general efficiency is increased.

Modern beekeeping also includes environmentally beneficial methods such as organic beekeeping, farming that is good for pollinators, and habitat preservation. Beekeepers are growing more conscious of the need for ecosystem health and biodiversity to ensure the long-term survival of bee populations.

All things considered, contemporary beekeeping advances highlight the industry's dedication to ongoing development, environmental care, and the welfare of honeybee colonies worldwide.

Chapter 11
<u>Troubleshooting And Frequently Asked Questions</u>

Troubleshooting and Common Challenges in Beekeeping cover a broad range of problems that beekeepers may run across in their work. Maintaining healthy and productive bee colonies requires skillful navigation of many obstacles, from controlling pests and predators to handling beehive problems and addressing beekeeper issues.

Controlling insects and predators that can endanger bee colonies is one of the biggest problems beekeepers have. Parasite pests called varroa mites, for instance, can damage bees by feeding on their body fluids and spreading diseases. To reduce varroa mite infestations while using fewer chemical treatments that might be harmful to bees and the environment, beekeepers must put into practice efficient methods like integrated pest management (IPM) procedures.

Managing predators that feed on bees, such as raccoons, skunks, and bears, is another typical problem. Bee populations can be upset and beehives are damaged by these creatures. To dissuade predators and protect their hives, beekeepers must take preventative steps like erecting electric fences.

A further essential component of beekeeping troubleshooting is beehive management. In hive management, colony strength is evaluated, hive health is tracked, and bee habitat and ventilation are provided. Regularly looking for illness, pests, or overcrowding, beekeepers must take quick remedial action to stop problems from getting worse.

Taking care of the many hurdles and roadblocks beekeepers could run against in their work is part of handling beekeeper issues. These difficulties may be anything from developing your beekeeping knowledge and skills to budgetary limitations and regulatory compliance. To successfully overcome these obstacles, beekeepers could need to attend workshops or training sessions, get assistance from local beekeeping societies, and keep up with industry best practices.

Troubleshooting and resolving typical beekeeping issues need a proactive and knowledgeable strategy. The long-term success of bee colonies can be promoted by beekeepers by putting into practice efficient pest and predator control techniques, quickly resolving beehive problems, and thoroughly addressing beekeeper difficulties.

Chapter 12

Succeeding Stories And Case Studies

Case studies and success stories from beekeepers provide insightful information about the trials, successes, and experiences of prosperous beekeepers. These anecdotes offer new and prospective beekeepers a plethora of information in addition to demonstrating the possibility of success in the field.

Profiles of Prosperous Bee Farmers

The variety of prosperous beekeepers and their paths to success are among the most motivating features of bee farming. Consider Sarah, a rural community beekeeper who made her love of bees her successful business. Sarah began with a small number of hives in her backyard and picked up the craft with practical experience and local beekeepers' mentoring. She gradually grew her business, putting into place environmentally friendly beekeeping methods and using technology to enhance hive management. Sarah is well-known today for the quality of her honey products, and her farm is an example of profitable and ecologically friendly beekeeping.

John's tale is another amazing one. He is a retired professional who found beekeeping to be a rewarding pastime. Though John had never worked in agriculture before, his commitment to studying bees and their habitat made him a well-liked bee farmer in his neighborhood. John learned everything from how to maintain hives to extract honey by trial and error. In beekeeping circles, he has won accolades and acclaim for his dedication to moral beekeeping practices including organic hive management and natural pest control techniques.

Top Practices and Lessons Learned:

Many times, the success tales of bee farmers include insightful advice and best practices that can help beekeepers of all skill levels. The need for ongoing education and adaptation in beekeeping is one important lesson. To be competitive in the business, successful bee farmers stress the significance of keeping up with bee health concerns, hive management methods, and market changes.

Regular attendance at conferences, workshops, and internet forums on beekeeping allows beekeepers to network with other enthusiasts and increase their knowledge.

Among the many facets of bee farming that are best practices are hive placement, hive maintenance, control of pests and diseases, and honey harvesting. Expert beekeepers emphasize the need to carefully select the site for bee colonies, taking into account things like sunshine exposure, closeness to feed sources, and weather protection. Good hive care, which includes routine health checks, enough ventilation, and cleanliness, benefits bee colonies generally and guarantees maximum honey output.

Sustainable beekeeping depends critically on efficient pest and disease control plans. Successful beekeepers support integrated pest management (IPM) methods that give natural remedies—including introducing helpful insects and applying non-toxic treatments—a priority when controlling pests like hive beetles and varroa mites. The mainstays of healthy bee populations are regular health monitoring, early disease detection, and quick action.

Inspirational Tales for Novice Beekeepers

Many times, new bee farmers look to seasoned beekeepers who have overcome obstacles and succeeded in the business for inspiration and direction. Motivational tales from seasoned bee growers show newbies the opportunities and benefits of beekeeping.

Take Maria, a young businesswoman who started beekeeping to foster sustainability and a connection with the natural world. Maria's love of bees and commitment to study carried her through the early difficulties, which included little money and knowledge. Under the guidance of seasoned beekeepers and emphasizing environmentally sustainable methods, Maria became a leader in urban beekeeping. Other young farmers are motivated to follow their passion for beekeeping and support environmental conservation initiatives by her narrative.

James, a beekeeper whose goal it is to use beekeeping to empower and educate underprivileged communities, has another uplifting story. James began his career by teaching locals beekeeping skills and hive management at a modest beekeeping project in a rural community. James turned the town into a beekeeping hub by working together and involving the community, creating sustainable jobs, and encouraging the preservation of nature. Aiming beekeepers hoping to use bee husbandry and community development to improve the world will find resonance in his experience.

Finally, beekeepers of all skill levels can learn a great deal and find inspiration from case studies and success stories. The various routes to success, the lessons discovered, and the finest methods in beekeeping are highlighted in the profiles of prosperous bee farmers. Encouragement stories for aspiring beekeepers inspire people to start their beekeeping adventure with zeal, tenacity, and a dedication to environmentally friendly methods.

Summary

We have covered every facet of this worthwhile and necessary activity in this thorough guide to beekeeping. For both novice and seasoned beekeepers, this book provides a comprehensive resource from comprehending the value and advantages of beekeeping to investigating possible markets for bee products.

The fundamentals of getting started—including selecting the appropriate bee species, establishing your bee farm, and acquiring the necessary beekeeping equipment—have been covered. For you to manage your hives successfully, you must understand bee biology and behavior. To that end, we have included information on bee anatomy, lifecycle, and hive behavior.

Important topics discussed in the hive management section are swarm prevention and management, as well as methods for hive inspection and maintenance.

The best bee health and productivity are ensured by careful attention to bee diet and feeding techniques.

Examining bee products including honey, beeswax, propolis, and pollen, we've talked about collecting, processing, and packaging methods. Additionally covered are frequent ailments, ways to prevent them, and available treatments for bee health and disease control.

We've included details on organic techniques, environmental factors, and integrated pest management plans for sustainable beekeeping practices. Expanding your bee farm covers scaling up production, diversifying bee products, and marketing techniques.

To help you keep informed about the most recent advancements in the field, advanced methods and technologies including queen bee rearing, bee breeding programs, and contemporary beekeeping advances are covered.

To give you the skills to get beyond beekeeping hurdles, troubleshooting typical problems, handling pests and predators, and handling beekeeper-related problems are covered.

Lastly, we have provided case studies and success stories that include the biographies of prosperous bee farmers together with best practices, lessons discovered, and inspirational tales to encourage aspiring beekeepers.

metabolisms, such as endomorphs, who often encounter challenges in weight management. By steering clear of a consistent dietary routine, Metabolic Confusion mitigates the risk of the body reducing its metabolic rate in response to prolonged calorie deficits. Rather than entering a state of metabolic slowdown, the body remains responsive, ensuring the sustained effectiveness of calorie burning over time.

Metabolic Confusion encompasses cyclic alterations in caloric intake, macronutrient ratios, and meal timing. This deliberate variation stimulates positive adaptations within the body, fostering enhanced metabolic efficiency. The cyclical nature of these changes serves as a powerful tool, encouraging the body to adapt positively to shifting dietary patterns. This not only supports more efficient calorie burning but also contributes to sustainable weight loss or maintenance.

In essence, Metabolic Confusion represents a nuanced and effective strategy that harnesses the body's adaptability to dietary stimuli, promoting a dynamic metabolic state that enhances efficiency and resilience in the pursuit of long-term weight management goals.

How the Diet Benefits Endomorph Women

Metabolic health holds profound significance for women, influencing various aspects of their well-being. Beyond the conventional focus on weight management, a well-functioning metabolism plays a pivotal role in hormonal balance, energy levels, and overall vitality.

In the context of women's unique physiological experiences, such as menstruation, pregnancy, and menopause, metabolic health becomes a key determinant of hormonal harmony. A balanced metabolism contributes to the regulation of estrogen and progesterone, which, in turn, can impact menstrual regularity, fertility, and the overall reproductive health of women.

Energy levels are intricately linked to metabolic health, and for women juggling multifaceted roles in daily life, maintaining optimal energy is paramount. A well-regulated metabolism ensures efficient energy utilization, supporting sustained physical and mental performance throughout the day.

Beyond the physical aspects, metabolic health significantly influences mood, cognitive function, and emotional well-being in women. Fluctuations in blood sugar levels, often associated with metabolic imbalances, can contribute to mood swings, fatigue, and difficulty concentrating. A stable and well-functioning metabolism aids in stabilizing these aspects, fostering a sense of mental clarity and emotional resilience.

Moreover, metabolic health plays a crucial role in the prevention of chronic diseases that disproportionately affect women, such as polycystic ovary syndrome (PCOS) and gestational diabetes. A proactive approach to maintaining metabolic health can mitigate the risk of these conditions, promoting long-term well-being.

In essence, the significance of metabolic health for women extends far beyond its superficial association with weight management. It is a fundamental element that intricately weaves into the fabric of women's overall health, influencing hormonal balance, energy levels, emotional wellness, and the prevention of chronic conditions. Prioritizing metabolic health emerges as a holistic and empowering endeavor, ensuring that women can navigate the various stages of life with resilience, vitality, and sustained well-being

Chapter 2

Metabolic Basics

the Science of Metabolism

The science of metabolism is a multifaceted and intricate exploration of the body's intricate biochemical processes that govern energy production, utilization, and storage. At its core, metabolism encompasses the totality of chemical reactions that occur within cells to sustain life, with a primary focus on how the body transforms and utilizes nutrients for energy.

Metabolism operates through two interconnected processes: catabolism and anabolism. Catabolism involves the breakdown of complex molecules, such as carbohydrates, fats, and proteins, into simpler compounds, releasing energy in the process.

Anabolism, on the other hand, encompasses the synthesis of complex molecules from simpler ones, requiring energy input.

Central to metabolic function is the role of enzymes, biological catalysts that facilitate and regulate the various chemical reactions within the body. Enzymes enable the efficient breakdown of nutrients during digestion and their subsequent utilization in cellular processes.

Energy metabolism, specifically, revolves around the conversion of food into energy currency units known as adenosine triphosphate (ATP). Carbohydrates, fats, and proteins are the primary macronutrients that undergo metabolic processes to produce ATP. Carbohydrates are broken down into glucose, fats into fatty acids, and proteins into amino acids, all of which enter the pathways leading to ATP production.

The concept of basal metabolic rate (BMR) further illustrates the individualized nature of metabolism. BMR represents the energy expended by the body at rest to maintain basic physiological functions such as breathing, circulation, and cell production. Factors influencing BMR include age, gender, body composition, and genetics, highlighting the intricate interplay of individual characteristics in metabolic processes.

The Impact of Hormones on Metabolic Function

Hormones play a crucial role in regulating metabolic function, influencing various physiological processes in the body. Metabolism refers to the complex set of chemical reactions that occur within cells to maintain life. Hormones are signaling molecules produced by endocrine glands, and they travel through the bloodstream to target organs or tissues, where they exert their effects.

Here are some key hormones that significantly impact metabolic function:

Insulin:

Produced by the pancreas, insulin plays a central role in glucose metabolism. It facilitates the uptake of glucose by cells, especially muscle and adipose (fat) cells, and promotes its storage as glycogen in the liver and muscles. Insulin also inhibits the breakdown of stored glycogen and stimulates the synthesis of fats.

Glucagon:

Also produced by the pancreas, but with opposite effects to insulin. Glucagon stimulates the breakdown of glycogen in the liver, releasing glucose into the bloodstream. This process, known as glycogenolysis, helps maintain blood glucose levels during periods of fasting or between meals.

Cortisol:

Produced by the adrenal glands, cortisol is often referred to as the "stress hormone." It plays a role in glucose metabolism by promoting gluconeogenesis, the synthesis of glucose from non-carbohydrate sources (such as amino acids). Cortisol also has anti-inflammatory effects and can mobilize energy stores during stress.

Thyroid Hormones (T3 and T4):

Thyroid hormones influence the basal metabolic rate (BMR), which is the amount of energy expended at rest. They affect the metabolism of carbohydrates, fats, and proteins, and their levels influence overall energy balance. An imbalance in thyroid hormones can lead to changes in weight and energy levels.

Leptin:

Produced by adipose tissue, leptin plays a role in appetite regulation and energy balance. It signals the brain when fat stores are sufficient, suppressing appetite and increasing energy expenditure. Leptin resistance can contribute to obesity.

Ghrelin:

Ghrelin is produced in the stomach and stimulates appetite. It acts in opposition to leptin, promoting food intake and influencing energy balance. Ghrelin levels typically rise before meals and decrease after eating.

Testosterone and Estrogen:

Sex hormones, including testosterone (predominantly in males) and estrogen (predominantly in females), influence body composition, fat distribution, and muscle mass. Changes in these hormones can impact metabolism and energy expenditure.

Imbalances in hormone levels, whether due to medical conditions, lifestyle factors, or aging, can lead to metabolic disorders such as diabetes, obesity, or thyroid dysfunction. Understanding the interplay between hormones and metabolic function is crucial for maintaining overall health and preventing metabolic-related disorders. Lifestyle factors, including diet, exercise, and stress management, can also influence hormone levels and metabolic health

Chapter 3

Weight Training for Fat Loss and Lean Muscle Mass

Effective Weight Training Techniques for Women

Weight training can be a highly effective and beneficial form of exercise for women. It not only helps in building and toning muscles but also contributes to improved metabolism, bone density, and overall strength.

Here are some effective weight training techniques for women:

1. **Start with Compound Exercises:**

Compound exercises work for multiple muscle groups at once, providing efficient and effective workouts. Examples include squats, deadlifts, lunges, bench presses, and overhead presses.

2. **Use Proper Form:**

Focus on maintaining proper form during each exercise to prevent injuries and maximize effectiveness. Consider working with a certified trainer, especially when starting, to ensure you're performing exercises correctly.

3. **Progressive Overload:**

Gradually increase the resistance (weight) you lift to challenge your muscles and promote strength gains. Progressive overload is a fundamental principle for building muscle and increasing overall strength.

4. **Include Bodyweight Exercises:**

Incorporate bodyweight exercises, such as push-ups, pull-ups, and planks, into your routine. These exercises help improve overall strength and stability.

5. **Adjustable Dumbbells:**

Consider using adjustable dumbbells, which allow you to vary the resistance for different exercises. This flexibility is especially useful for home workouts.

6. **High-Intensity Interval Training (HIIT):**

Combine weight training with high-intensity interval training for a time-efficient and effective workout. This approach can boost calorie burn, improve cardiovascular health, and enhance overall fitness.

7. **Include Core Exercises:**

Strengthening the core is essential for stability and overall strength. Include exercises such as planks, Russian twists, and leg raises to target the abdominal muscles.

8. **Balanced Training Program:**

Design a balanced program that targets all major muscle groups. This helps prevent muscle imbalances and ensures overall strength and functionality.

9. **Focus on Functional Movements:**

Include exercises that mimic real-life movements, such as squats and lunges, to improve overall functional fitness.

10. **Rest and Recovery:**

Allow your muscles time to recover by incorporating rest days into your routine. This is when muscle repair and growth occur.

11. **Consistency is Key:**

Consistency is crucial for seeing results. Aim for a regular weight training routine, and gradually increase the intensity and duration over time.

12. **Listen to Your Body:**

Pay attention to how your body responds to exercise. If you experience pain (beyond typical muscle soreness), adjust your routine or seek guidance from a fitness professional.

Building Strength and Toning for Metabolic Enhancement

Building strength and toning muscles are excellent strategies for metabolic enhancement. Muscle tissue is metabolically active, meaning it burns more calories at rest compared to fat tissue. As you increase your muscle mass through strength training, you can positively impact your metabolism and contribute to better overall metabolic health.

Here are some key tips for building strength, toning muscles, and enhancing metabolism:

1. **Incorporate Resistance Training:**

Include both weightlifting and bodyweight exercises in your workout routine. Focus on compound movements like squats, deadlifts, bench presses, and rows to engage multiple muscle groups simultaneously.

2. **Progressive Overload:**

Gradually increase the resistance or intensity of your workouts to challenge your muscles and stimulate growth. This can involve adding more weight, increasing the number of repetitions, or adjusting rest intervals.

3. **Include High-Intensity Interval Training (HIIT):**

Integrate HIIT workouts into your routine to elevate your heart rate and maximize calorie burn. HIIT has been shown to enhance both aerobic and anaerobic fitness, contributing to metabolic improvements.

4. **Combine Strength Training with Cardio:**

While strength training is crucial, incorporating cardiovascular exercises can contribute to overall metabolic health. Find a balance that suits your preferences and fitness goals.

5. **Focus on Large Muscle Groups:**

Targeting large muscle groups, such as those in the legs and back, can result in a more significant calorie burn both during and after your workout.

6. **Short Rest Intervals:**

Keep rest intervals relatively short between sets to maintain an elevated heart rate and increase the overall intensity of your workout.

7. **Include Core Exercises:**

A strong core is essential for stability and overall strength. Include exercises such as planks, Russian twists, and leg raises to target the abdominal muscles.

8. **Vary Your Workouts:**

Avoid monotony by incorporating variety into your workouts. This not only keeps things interesting but also challenges your body in different ways, promoting well-rounded strength and toning.

9. **Nutrition Matters:**

Consume a balanced diet that supports your fitness goals. Ensure an adequate intake of protein to support muscle growth and repair. Consider consulting with a nutritionist to tailor your diet to your specific needs.

10. **Adequate Protein Intake:**

Protein is essential for muscle repair and growth. Aim for a protein-rich diet, including lean meats, fish, dairy, legumes, and plant-based protein sources.

11. **Stay Hydrated:**

Proper hydration is crucial for overall health and can support optimal exercise performance and recovery.

12. **Prioritize Sleep:**

Quality sleep is essential for muscle recovery and overall well-being. Aim for 7-9 hours of sleep per night to support your body's regeneration processes.

Chapter 4

28-day Meal Plan for Metabolic Confusion

Day 1:

Breakfast: Scrambled eggs with spinach and whole-grain toast.

Lunch: Grilled chicken salad with mixed greens, cherry tomatoes, cucumbers, and balsamic vinaigrette.

Snack: Greek yogurt with mixed berries.

Dinner: Baked salmon with quinoa and steamed broccoli.

Dessert: Mixed fruit salad.

Day 2:

Breakfast: Overnight oats with almond milk, chia seeds, sliced banana, and a sprinkle of cinnamon.

Lunch: Turkey and avocado wrap with whole-grain tortilla.

Snack: Carrot and celery sticks with hummus.

Dinner: Stir-fried tofu with assorted vegetables and brown rice.

Dessert: Dark chocolate squares.

Day 3:

Breakfast: Smoothie with spinach, frozen berries, banana, almond milk, and a scoop of protein powder.

Lunch: Lentil soup with whole-grain roll.

Snack: Handful of mixed nuts.

Dinner: Grilled lean steak with roasted sweet potatoes and asparagus.

Dessert: Baked apple with a sprinkle of cinnamon.

Day 4:

Breakfast: Cottage cheese with sliced peaches and a drizzle of honey.

Lunch: Quinoa salad with black beans, corn, bell peppers, and lime vinaigrette.

Snack: Rice cakes with almond butter.

Dinner: Baked chicken breast with cauliflower rice and sautéed zucchini.

Dessert: Yogurt parfait with granola and sliced strawberries.

Day 5:

Breakfast: Whole-grain pancakes with mixed berries and a dollop of Greek yogurt.

Lunch: Spinach and feta stuffed chicken breast with a side salad.

Snack: Sliced apple with peanut butter.

Dinner: Grilled fish tacos with cabbage slaw and avocado.

Dessert: Frozen banana slices dipped in dark chocolate.

Day 6:

Breakfast: Scrambled egg whites with spinach and whole-grain toast.

Lunch: Chickpea and vegetable stir-fry with brown rice.

Snack: Sliced cucumber with tzatziki sauce.

Dinner: Baked cod with quinoa and roasted Brussels sprouts.

Dessert: Mixed berries with a dollop of whipped cream.

Day 7:

Breakfast: Greek yogurt parfait with granola and mixed fruits.

Lunch: Grilled portobello mushroom burger with a side salad.

Snack: Trail mix with nuts, dried fruits, and seeds.

Dinner: Stir-fried shrimp with broccoli and cauliflower rice.

Dessert: Chia seed pudding with mango chunks.

Day 8:

Breakfast: Whole-grain waffles topped with almond butter and sliced strawberries.

Lunch: Mediterranean-style wrap with hummus, roasted red peppers, and greens.

Snack: Edamame pods sprinkled with sea salt.

Dinner: Baked turkey meatballs with zucchini noodles and marinara sauce.

Dessert: Fresh pineapple slices.

Day 9:

Breakfast: Omelette with mushrooms, onions, and bell peppers.

Lunch: Quinoa and black bean stuffed bell peppers.

Snack: Cottage cheese with pineapple chunks.

Dinner: Grilled vegetables and tofu kebabs with couscous.

Dessert: Mixed berry smoothie bowl with granola.

Day 10:

Breakfast: Peanut butter and banana smoothie with a scoop of protein powder.

Lunch: Tuna salad lettuce wraps with a side of carrot sticks.

Snack: Rice cakes with cottage cheese and sliced strawberries.

Dinner: Baked chicken thighs with roasted sweet potatoes and green beans.

Dessert: Frozen yogurt popsicles.

Day 11:

Breakfast: Spinach and mushroom frittata.

Lunch: Quinoa and roasted vegetable bowl with a drizzle of tahini.

Snack: Apple slices with almond butter.

Dinner: Baked salmon with wild rice and steamed asparagus.

Dessert: Mixed fruit kabobs.

Day 12:

Breakfast: Cottage cheese and fruit bowl.

Lunch: Grilled chicken Caesar salad with whole-grain croutons.

Snack: Mixed nuts and dried cranberries.

Dinner: Beef and vegetable stir-fry with brown rice.

Dessert: Baked pear with a sprinkle of cinnamon.

Day 13:

Breakfast: Oatmeal topped with sliced almonds and diced apples.

Lunch: Lentil and vegetable curry with a side of naan bread.

Snack: Baby carrots with guacamole.

Dinner: Stuffed acorn squash with ground turkey and quinoa stuffing.

Dessert: Berries with a drizzle of honey and chopped mint.

Day 14:

Breakfast: Greek yogurt with honey and walnuts.

Lunch: Turkey and avocado lettuce wrap with a side of mixed berries.

Snack: Rice cakes with hummus and cherry tomatoes.

Dinner: Grilled shrimp with sweet potato wedges and broccoli.

Dessert: Dark chocolate-covered strawberries.

Day 15:

Breakfast: Whole-grain pancakes with mixed berries and a dollop of yogurt.

Lunch: Chickpea and vegetable salad with lemon-tahini dressing.

Snack: Sliced bell peppers with hummus.

Dinner: Baked chicken breast with quinoa and sautéed spinach.

Dessert: Baked apple chips.

Day 16:

Breakfast: Scrambled eggs with sautéed spinach and whole-grain toast.

Lunch: Quinoa and black bean salad with corn, tomatoes, and lime dressing.

Snack: Mixed nuts and a small apple.

Dinner: Grilled vegetables and chicken skewers with couscous.

Dessert: Greek yogurt with a drizzle of honey and sliced almonds.

Day 17:

Breakfast: Smoothie with kale, banana, frozen berries, and almond milk.

Lunch: Tofu and vegetable stir-fry with brown rice.

Snack: Baby carrots with hummus.

Dinner: Baked cod with mashed sweet potatoes and green beans.

Dessert: Sliced melon with a sprinkle of lime zest.

Day 18:

Breakfast: Overnight chia seed pudding with mixed berries.

Lunch: Turkey and vegetable wrap with a side salad.

Snack: Cottage cheese with pineapple.

Dinner: Lentil and vegetable stew with whole-grain bread.

Dessert: Dark chocolate-covered almonds.

Day 19:

Breakfast: Whole-grain waffles topped with Greek yogurt and sliced peaches.

Lunch: Chickpea and avocado salad with lemon-tahini dressing.

Snack: Rice cakes with almond butter and banana slices.

Dinner: Grilled steak with roasted potatoes and broccoli.

Dessert: Baked cinnamon banana boats.

Day 20:

Breakfast: Scrambled egg whites with diced tomatoes and whole-grain toast.

Lunch: Spinach and feta stuffed bell peppers.

Snack: Mixed berries with a handful of granola.

Dinner: Baked chicken thighs with quinoa and roasted Brussels sprouts.

Dessert: Frozen yogurt with sliced strawberries.

Day 21:

Breakfast: Greek yogurt with mixed berries and a sprinkle of granola.

Lunch: Grilled vegetables and quinoa-stuffed portobello mushrooms.

Snack: Celery sticks with peanut butter.

Dinner: Baked salmon with wild rice and steamed broccoli.

Dessert: Sliced mango with a drizzle of lime juice.

Day 22:

Breakfast: Smoothie with spinach, banana, almond milk, and a scoop of protein powder.

Lunch: Tofu and vegetable noodle stir-fry.

Snack: Handful of trail mix with dried fruits and nuts.

Dinner: Baked chicken breast with roasted sweet potatoes and asparagus.

Dessert: Chia seed and coconut milk pudding.

Day 23:

Breakfast: Oatmeal with diced apples, walnuts, and a touch of cinnamon.

Lunch: Lentil and vegetable wrap with hummus.

Snack: Sliced cucumber with tzatziki sauce.

Dinner: Grilled shrimp with quinoa and sautéed spinach.

Dessert: Frozen banana pops coated in crushed nuts.

Day 24:

Breakfast: Scrambled eggs with diced tomatoes and a whole-grain English muffin.

Lunch: Turkey and avocado lettuce wrap with a side of mixed berries.

Snack: Rice cakes with almond butter and sliced strawberries.

Dinner: Baked cod with mashed sweet potatoes and green beans.

Dessert: Dark chocolate-dipped orange segments.

Day 25:

Breakfast: Whole-grain pancakes with mixed berries and Greek yogurt.

Lunch: Chickpea and vegetable salad with lemon-tahini dressing.

Snack: Baby carrots with hummus.

Dinner: Grilled steak with roasted potatoes and broccoli.

Dessert: Mixed fruit salad with a sprinkle of mint.

Day 26:

Breakfast: Scrambled egg whites with sautéed spinach and whole-grain toast.

Lunch: Quinoa and black bean salad with corn, tomatoes, and lime dressing.

Snack: Mixed nuts and a small apple.

Dinner: Grilled vegetables and chicken skewers with couscous.

Dessert: Greek yogurt with a drizzle of honey and sliced almonds.

Day 27:

Breakfast: Smoothie with kale, banana, frozen berries, and almond milk.

Lunch: Tofu and vegetable stir-fry with brown rice.

Snack: Baby carrots with hummus.

Dinner: Baked cod with mashed sweet potatoes and green beans.

Dessert: Sliced melon with a sprinkle of lime zest.

Day 28:

Breakfast: Overnight chia seed pudding with mixed berries.

Lunch: Turkey and vegetable wrap with a side salad.

Snack: Cottage cheese with pineapple.

Dinner: Lentil and vegetable stew with whole-grain bread.

Dessert: Dark chocolate-covered almonds.

Chapter 5

Breakfast recipes for metabolic confusion

Quinoa Breakfast Bowl

Ingredients:

- 1 cup cooked quinoa

- 1/2 cup Greek yogurt

- 1/4 cup mixed berries

- 1 tablespoon honey

- 1 tablespoon chopped nuts

Instructions:

1. In a bowl, combine cooked quinoa and Greek yogurt.

2. Top with mixed berries, drizzle with honey and sprinkle with chopped nuts.

Nutritional Information:

- Calories: 350

- Protein: 15g

- Carbohydrates: 55g

- Fat: 8g

Sweet Potato and Black Bean Breakfast Wrap

Ingredients:

- 1 whole-grain tortilla

- 1/2 cup mashed sweet potato

- 1/4 cup black beans (canned, drained, and rinsed)

- 1 egg, scrambled

- Salsa and avocado slices (optional)

Instructions:

1. Spread mashed sweet potato on the tortilla.

2. Add black beans and scrambled egg.

3. Roll into a wrap and, if desired, top with salsa and avocado slices.

Nutritional Information:

- Calories: 380

- Protein: 17g

- Carbohydrates: 55g

- Fat: 12g

Chia Seed Pudding Parfait

Ingredients:

- 2 tablespoons chia seeds

- 1/2 cup almond milk

- 1/4 cup granola

- 1/2 cup mixed fruit (e.g., berries and kiwi)

Instructions:

1. Mix chia seeds and almond milk, and let it sit in the fridge for at least 2 hours or overnight.

2. Layer chia pudding with granola and mixed fruit in a glass.

Nutritional Information:

- Calories: 320

- Protein: 8g

- Carbohydrates: 45g

- Fat: 14g

Egg and Vegetable Breakfast Stir-Fry

Ingredients:

- 2 eggs, beaten

- 1 cup mixed vegetables (bell peppers, spinach, tomatoes)

- 1 teaspoon olive oil

- Salt and pepper to taste

Instructions:

1. Heat olive oil in a pan, sauté mixed vegetables until tender.

2. Pour beaten eggs over vegetables, and scramble until cooked.

3. Season with salt and pepper.

Nutritional Information:

- Calories: 280

- Protein: 14g

- Carbohydrates: 10g

- Fat: 20g

Cottage Cheese and Pineapple Bowl

Ingredients:

- 1 cup low-fat cottage cheese

- 1/2 cup fresh pineapple chunks

- 1 tablespoon flaxseeds

- Drizzle of honey

Instructions:

1. In a bowl, combine cottage cheese and pineapple.

2. Sprinkle with flaxseeds and drizzle with honey.

Nutritional Information:

- Calories: 260

- Protein: 28g

- Carbohydrates: 20g

- Fat: 8g

Oatmeal with Nut Butter and Banana

Ingredients:

- 1/2 cup rolled oats

- 1 cup almond milk

- 1 tablespoon almond butter

- 1 banana, sliced

Instructions:

1. Cook oats with almond milk until creamy.

2. Top with almond butter and banana slices.

Nutritional Information:

- Calories: 380

- Protein: 12g

- Carbohydrates: 55g

- Fat: 15g

Mediterranean Egg Muffins

Ingredients:

- 2 eggs, beaten

- Cherry tomatoes, olives, and feta cheese

- Fresh basil, chopped

Instructions:

1. Preheat oven to 350°F (175°C).

2. Mix beaten eggs with tomatoes, olives, and feta.

3. Pour into muffin tin, sprinkle with fresh basil, and bake for 15-20 minutes.

Nutritional Information:

- Calories: 220

- Protein: 15g

- Carbohydrates: 5g

- Fat: 15g

Green Smoothie Bowl

Ingredients:

- 1 cup spinach

- 1/2 banana

- 1/2 cup pineapple chunks

- 1/2 cup Greek yogurt

- 1 tablespoon chia seeds

Instructions:

1. Blend spinach, banana, pineapple, and Greek yogurt until smooth.

2. Pour into a bowl and top with chia seeds.

Nutritional Information:

- Calories: 290

- Protein: 15g

- Carbohydrates: 45g

- Fat: 8g

Turkey and Vegetable Breakfast Skillet

Ingredients:

- 3 ounces lean ground turkey

- 1 cup diced vegetables (bell peppers, zucchini, onions)

- 2 eggs

- Salt and pepper to taste

Instructions:

1. Cook ground turkey in a skillet until browned.

2. Add diced vegetables and cook until tender.

3. Crack eggs into the skillet, and scramble until cooked.

4. Season with salt and pepper.

Nutritional Information:

- Calories: 320

- Protein: 25g

- Carbohydrates: 10g

- Fat: 18g

Cocoa and Banana Protein Smoothie

Ingredients:

- 1 scoop of chocolate protein powder

- 1 cup almond milk

- 1/2 banana

- 1 tablespoon almond butter

- Ice cubes

Instructions:

1. Blend protein powder, almond milk, banana, and almond butter until smooth.

2. Add ice cubes and blend again.

Nutritional Information:

- Calories: 300

- Protein: 25g

- Carbohydrates: 25g

- Fat: 12g

Salmon and Avocado Toast

Ingredients:

- 2 slices whole-grain bread

- 3 ounces smoked salmon

- 1/2 avocado, sliced

- Lemon juice and dill for garnish

Instructions:

1. Toast whole-grain bread slices.

2. Top with smoked salmon and sliced avocado.

3. Drizzle with lemon juice and garnish with dill.

Nutritional Information:

- Calories: 320

- Protein: 20g

- Carbohydrates: 25g

- Fat: 15g

Blueberry and Almond Overnight Oats

Ingredients:

- 1/2 cup rolled oats

- 1/2 cup almond milk

- 1/4 cup blueberries

- 1 tablespoon almond slices

- 1 teaspoon honey

Instructions:

1. Mix rolled oats and almond milk in a jar.

2. Add blueberries, almond slices, and honey.

3. Refrigerate overnight and enjoy in the morning.

Nutritional Information:

- Calories: 280

- Protein: 8g

- Carbohydrates: 45g

- Fat: 10g

Vegetarian Breakfast Burrito

Ingredients:

- 1 whole-grain tortilla

- 1/2 cup black beans (canned, drained, and rinsed)

- Scrambled tofu or eggs

- Salsa, avocado, and cilantro for topping

Instructions:

1. Warm the tortilla.

2. Fill with black beans and scrambled tofu or eggs.

3. Top with salsa, avocado, and cilantro.

Nutritional Information:

- Calories: 350

- Protein: 18g

- Carbohydrates: 40g

- Fat: 15g

Peanut Butter Banana Protein Pancakes

Ingredients:

- 1 cup whole-grain pancake mix

- 1 scoop vanilla protein powder

- 1/2 cup almond milk

- 1 banana, mashed

- 1 tablespoon peanut butter

Instructions:

1. Mix pancake mix, protein powder, almond milk, and mashed banana.

2. Cook pancakes on a griddle.

3. Top with a dollop of peanut butter.

Nutritional Information:

- Calories: 400

- Protein: 20g

- Carbohydrates: 50g

- Fat: 15g

Egg White Veggie Omelette

Ingredients:

- 3 egg whites

- 1/2 cup diced vegetables (bell peppers, tomatoes, spinach)

- 1 tablespoon feta cheese

- Fresh herbs (parsley, chives) for garnish

Instructions:

1. Whisk egg whites and pour into a heated non-stick skillet.

2. Add diced vegetables and feta cheese.

3. Fold into an omelette and garnish with fresh herbs.

Nutritional Information:

- Calories: 150

- Protein: 20g

- Carbohydrates: 5g

- Fat: 5g

Chapter 6

Lunch recipes for metabolic confusion

Grilled Chicken and Quinoa Salad

Ingredients:

- 4 oz grilled chicken breast
- 1 cup cooked quinoa
- Mixed greens
- Cherry tomatoes
- Cucumber slices
- Balsamic vinaigrette

Instructions:

1. Slice grilled chicken.

2. Combine quinoa, mixed greens, cherry tomatoes, cucumber slices, and grilled chicken.

3. Drizzle with balsamic vinaigrette.

Nutritional Information:

- Calories: 400

- Protein: 30g

- Carbohydrates: 30g

- Fat: 18g

Vegetarian Chickpea Stir-Fry

Ingredients:

- 1 cup cooked chickpeas

- Mixed vegetables (broccoli, bell peppers, carrots)

- 1 cup brown rice

- 2 tablespoons soy sauce

- 1 tablespoon sesame oil

Instructions:

1. Sauté mixed vegetables in sesame oil.

2. Add cooked chickpeas and soy sauce.

3. Serve over brown rice.

Nutritional Information:

- Calories: 380

- Protein: 15g

- Carbohydrates: 60g

- Fat: 10g

Salmon and Quinoa Bowl

Ingredients:

- 4 oz baked salmon

- 1 cup cooked quinoa

- Steamed broccoli

- Avocado slices

- Lemon tahini dressing

Instructions:

1. Flake baked salmon.

2. Combine quinoa, steamed broccoli, avocado slices, and salmon.

3. Drizzle with lemon tahini dressing.

Nutritional Information:

- Calories: 420

- Protein: 30g

- Carbohydrates: 35g

- Fat: 18g

Turkey and Vegetable Wrap

Ingredients:

- 4 oz lean ground turkey, cooked

- Whole-grain wrap

- Lettuce, tomato, and cucumber slices

- Greek yogurt dressing

Instructions:

1. Fill a whole-grain wrap with cooked ground turkey, lettuce, tomato, and cucumber slices.

2. Drizzle with Greek yogurt dressing.

Nutritional Information:

- Calories: 350

- Protein: 25g

- Carbohydrates: 30g

- Fat: 15g

Quinoa and Black Bean Salad

Ingredients:

- 1 cup cooked quinoa

- 1/2 cup black beans (canned, drained, and rinsed)

- Corn kernels

- Diced bell peppers

- Lime vinaigrette

Instructions:

1. Mix cooked quinoa, black beans, corn, and diced bell peppers.

2. Drizzle with lime vinaigrette.

Nutritional Information:

- Calories: 320

- Protein: 12g

- Carbohydrates: 55g

- Fat: 8g

Shrimp and Zucchini Noodles

Ingredients:

- 4 oz shrimp, cooked

- Zucchini noodles

- Cherry tomatoes

- Garlic, minced

- Olive oil

Instructions:

1. Sauté shrimp and minced garlic in olive oil.

2. Add zucchini noodles and cherry tomatoes.

3. Cook until noodles are tender.

Nutritional Information:

- Calories: 280

- Protein: 25g

- Carbohydrates: 15g

- Fat: 14g

Caprese Chicken Salad

Ingredients:

- 4 oz grilled chicken breast

- Mixed greens

- Cherry tomatoes

- Fresh mozzarella

- Balsamic glaze

Instructions:

1. Slice grilled chicken and fresh mozzarella.

2. Combine mixed greens, cherry tomatoes, chicken, and mozzarella.

3. Drizzle with balsamic glaze.

Nutritional Information:

- Calories: 350

- Protein: 30g

- Carbohydrates: 10g

- Fat: 18g

Vegetable and Tofu Stir-Fry

Ingredients:

- 1 cup tofu, cubed

- Mixed vegetables (broccoli, snow peas, carrots)

- Brown rice

- Soy ginger sauce

Instructions:

1. Sauté tofu and mixed vegetables.

2. Add soy-ginger sauce and cook until vegetables are tender.

3. Serve over brown rice.

Nutritional Information:

- Calories: 380

- Protein: 20g

- Carbohydrates: 45g

- Fat: 15g

Mediterranean Chickpea Salad

Ingredients:

- 1 cup canned chickpeas, drained and rinsed

- Cucumber, diced

- Cherry tomatoes, halved

- Red onion, finely chopped

- Feta cheese

- Olive oil and lemon dressing

Instructions:

1. Combine chickpeas, cucumber, cherry tomatoes, red onion, and feta cheese.

2. Drizzle with olive oil and lemon dressing.

Nutritional Information:

- Calories: 320

- Protein: 15g

- Carbohydrates: 45g

- Fat: 12g

Tuna and Avocado Wrap

Ingredients:

- 1 can tuna, drained

- Whole-grain wrap

- Avocado, sliced

- Spinach leaves

- Greek yogurt or mustard for dressing

Instructions:

1. Mix tuna with Greek yogurt or mustard.

2. Fill a whole-grain wrap with tuna, sliced avocado, and spinach leaves.

Nutritional Information:

- Calories: 340

- Protein: 25g

- Carbohydrates: 30g

- Fat: 15g

Chicken and Vegetable Quinoa Bowl

Ingredients:

- 4 oz grilled chicken breast

- 1 cup cooked quinoa

- Steamed broccoli and cauliflower

- Hummus for topping

Instructions:

1. Slice grilled chicken.

2. Combine quinoa, steamed broccoli, and cauliflower.

3. Top with sliced chicken and a dollop of hummus.

Nutritional Information:

- Calories: 380

- Protein: 30g

- Carbohydrates: 40g

- Fat: 15g

Pesto Zoodles with Chicken

Ingredients:

- 4 oz grilled chicken breast

- Zucchini noodles (zoodles)

- Cherry tomatoes, halved

- Pesto sauce

Instructions:

1. Slice grilled chicken.

2. Sauté zucchini noodles until tender.

3. Toss zoodles with cherry tomatoes, grilled chicken, and pesto sauce.

Nutritional Information:

- Calories: 350

- Protein: 30g

- Carbohydrates: 10g

- Fat: 18g

Egg and Spinach Salad

Ingredients:

- 2 boiled eggs, sliced

- Baby spinach leaves

- Cherry tomatoes

- Avocado, diced

- Olive oil and balsamic vinegar

Instructions:

1. Arrange baby spinach on a plate.

2. Top with sliced boiled eggs, cherry tomatoes, and diced avocado.

3. Drizzle with olive oil and balsamic vinegar.

Nutritional Information:

- Calories: 320

- Protein: 15g

- Carbohydrates: 15g

- Fat: 20g

Black Bean and Vegetable Quesadilla

Ingredients:

- Whole-grain tortilla

- 1/2 cup black beans (canned, drained, and rinsed)

- Mixed vegetables (bell peppers, onions, corn)

- Shredded cheese

- Greek yogurt or salsa for dipping

Instructions:

1. Spread black beans on a whole-grain tortilla.

2. Top with mixed vegetables and shredded cheese.

3. Fold in half and cook until cheese melts.

4. Serve with Greek yogurt or salsa for dipping.

Nutritional Information:

- Calories: 360

- Protein: 15g

- Carbohydrates: 45g

- Fat: 15g

Teriyaki Chicken and Broccoli

Ingredients:

- 4 oz grilled chicken breast, sliced

- Steamed broccoli

- Brown rice

- Teriyaki sauce

Instructions:

1. Combine grilled chicken, steamed broccoli, and brown rice.

2. Drizzle with teriyaki sauce and toss to coat.

Nutritional Information:

- Calories: 400

- Protein: 30g

- Carbohydrates: 50g

- Fat: 10g

Chapter 7

Dinner recipes for metabolic confusion

Salmon and Asparagus Foil Packets

Ingredients:

- 6 oz salmon fillet

- Asparagus spears

- Lemon slices

- Olive oil

- Garlic powder

- Salt and pepper

Instructions:

1. Place salmon on a piece of foil, and surround it with asparagus.

2. Drizzle with olive oil, sprinkle with garlic powder, salt, and pepper.

3. Seal the foil and bake at 375°F (190°C) for 20 minutes.

Nutritional Information:

- Calories: 400

- Protein: 35g

- Carbohydrates: 10g

- Fat: 25g

Quinoa-Stuffed Bell Peppers

Ingredients:

- Bell peppers

- 1 cup cooked quinoa

- Black beans (canned, drained, and rinsed)

- Corn kernels

- Salsa

- Shredded cheese

Instructions:

1. Cut bell peppers in half, and remove seeds.

2. Mix quinoa, black beans, corn, and salsa.

3. Stuff peppers, top with shredded cheese, and bake at 350°F (175°C) for 25 minutes.

Nutritional Information:

- Calories: 380

- Protein: 15g

- Carbohydrates: 60g

- Fat: 10g

Chicken and Vegetable Stir-Fry

Ingredients:

- 6 oz chicken breast, sliced

- Mixed vegetables (broccoli, bell peppers, carrots)

- Soy sauce

- Ginger and garlic, minced

- Brown rice

Instructions:

1. Sauté chicken until cooked.

2. Add mixed vegetables, soy sauce, ginger, and garlic.

3. Serve over brown rice.

Nutritional Information:

- Calories: 420

- Protein: 30g

- Carbohydrates: 50g

- Fat: 10g

Vegetarian Lentil Soup

Ingredients:

- 1 cup lentils, rinsed

- Vegetable broth

- Carrots, celery, onions, diced

- Garlic, minced

- Cumin and coriander

- Spinach leaves

Instructions:

1. Sauté garlic, carrots, celery, and onions.

2. Add lentils, vegetable broth, cumin, and coriander.

3. Simmer until lentils are tender, then add spinach.

Nutritional Information:

- Calories: 320

- Protein: 18g

- Carbohydrates: 50g

- Fat: 5g

Baked Chicken and Sweet Potato

Ingredients:

- 6 oz chicken breast

- Sweet potatoes, sliced

- Olive oil

- Paprika, garlic powder, salt, and pepper

Instructions:

1. Coat chicken and sweet potato slices with olive oil.

2. Season with paprika, garlic powder, salt, and pepper.

3. Bake at 400°F (200°C) for 30-35 minutes.

Nutritional Information:

- Calories: 380

- Protein: 35g

- Carbohydrates: 30g

- Fat: 15g

Mushroom and Spinach Quiche

Ingredients:

- Whole-grain pie crust

- Eggs

- Milk or almond milk

- Mushrooms, sliced

- Fresh spinach

- Feta cheese

Instructions:

1. Whisk eggs and milk, and pour into pie crust.

2. Add mushrooms, spinach, and feta.

3. Bake at 375°F (190°C) for 30-35 minutes.

Nutritional Information:

- Calories: 350

- Protein: 20g

- Carbohydrates: 25g

- Fat: 18g

Shrimp and Broccoli Stir-Fry

Ingredients:

- 6 oz shrimp, peeled and deveined

- Broccoli florets

- Soy sauce

- Sesame oil

- Garlic and ginger, minced

- Brown rice

Instructions:

1. Sauté shrimp, garlic, and ginger in sesame oil.

2. Add broccoli and soy sauce.

3. Serve over brown rice.

Nutritional Information:

- Calories: 320

- Protein: 25g

- Carbohydrates: 40g

- Fat: 10g

Turkey and Quinoa Stuffed Peppers

Ingredients:

- Bell peppers

- Ground turkey

- Quinoa, cooked

- Diced tomatoes

- Black beans (canned, drained, and rinsed)

- Taco seasoning

Instructions:

1. Cut bell peppers in half, and remove seeds.

2. Brown ground turkey, mixed with quinoa, tomatoes, black beans, and taco seasoning.

3. Stuff peppers and bake at 375°F (190°C) for 25 minutes.

Nutritional Information:

- Calories: 380

- Protein: 25g

- Carbohydrates: 45g

- Fat: 12g

Salmon and Sweet Potato Skewers

Ingredients:

- 6 oz salmon fillet, cut into cubes

- Sweet potatoes, cubed

- Olive oil

- Dill, lemon juice, salt, and pepper

Instructions:

1. Thread salmon and sweet potato cubes onto skewers.

2. Brush with olive oil, and sprinkle with dill, lemon juice, salt, and pepper.

3. Grill for 10-12 minutes.

Nutritional Information:

- Calories: 420

- Protein: 30g

- Carbohydrates: 35g

- Fat: 20g

Vegetarian Chickpea Curry

Ingredients:

- 1 can chickpeas, drained and rinsed

- Coconut milk

- Diced tomatoes

- Onion, garlic, and ginger, minced

- Curry powder, cumin, and coriander

- Spinach leaves

Instructions:

1. Sauté onion, garlic, and ginger.

2. Add chickpeas, diced tomatoes, coconut milk, curry powder, cumin, and coriander.

3. Simmer until flavors meld, then add spinach.

Nutritional Information:

- Calories: 340

- Protein: 15g

- Carbohydrates: 40g

- Fat: 15g

Turkey and Vegetable Skillet

Ingredients:

- 6 oz ground turkey
- Bell peppers, onions, zucchini, diced
- Tomato sauce
- Italian seasoning, salt, and pepper
- Whole-grain pasta

Instructions:

1. Brown ground turkey, add diced vegetables, tomato sauce, Italian seasoning, salt, and pepper.
2. Simmer until vegetables are tender.
3. Serve over whole-grain pasta.

Nutritional Information:

- Calories: 400
- Protein: 25g

- Carbohydrates: 45g

- Fat: 15g

Cauliflower and Chickpea Curry

Ingredients:

- Cauliflower florets

- 1 can chickpeas, drained and rinsed

- Coconut milk

- Curry paste

- Onion, garlic, and ginger, minced

- Basmati rice

Instructions:

1. Sauté onion, garlic, and ginger.

2. Add cauliflower, chickpeas, coconut milk, and curry paste.

3. Simmer until cauliflower is tender.

4. Serve over basmati rice.

Nutritional Information:

- Calories: 350

- Protein: 15g

- Carbohydrates: 55g

- Fat: 10g

Lemon Garlic Herb Grilled Chicken

Ingredients:

- 6 oz chicken breast

- Lemon juice

- Garlic, minced

- Fresh herbs (rosemary, thyme, parsley)

- Olive oil

- Quinoa

Instructions:

1. Marinate chicken in lemon juice, minced garlic, fresh herbs, and olive oil.

2. Grill until cooked through.

3. Serve over quinoa.

Nutritional Information:

- Calories: 380

- Protein: 30g

- Carbohydrates: 30g

- Fat: 18g

Eggplant and Tomato Bake

Ingredients:

- Eggplant, sliced

- Roma tomatoes, sliced

- Mozzarella cheese

- Tomato sauce

- Italian seasoning, salt, and pepper

Instructions:

1. Layer eggplant and tomato slices in a baking dish.

2. Top with tomato sauce, mozzarella cheese, Italian seasoning, salt, and pepper.

3. Bake at 375°F (190°C) for 30-35 minutes.

Nutritional Information:

- Calories: 320

- Protein: 15g

- Carbohydrates: 30g

- Fat: 15g

Pesto and Tomato Chicken

Ingredients:

- 6 oz chicken breast

- Pesto sauce

- Cherry tomatoes, halved

- Whole-grain couscous

Instructions:

1. Coat chicken with pesto sauce.

2. Grill or bake until cooked through.

3. Serve over whole-grain couscous, topped with cherry tomatoes.

Nutritional Information:

- Calories: 400

- Protein: 30g

- Carbohydrates: 35g

- Fat: 18g

Chapter 8

Snack recipes for metabolic confusion

Apple Slices with Almond Butter

Ingredients:

- 1 medium apple, sliced

- 2 tablespoons almond butter

Instructions:

1. Spread almond butter on apple slices.

2. Enjoy as a satisfying and crunchy snack.

Nutritional Information:

- Calories: 200

- Protein: 5g

- Carbohydrates: 25g

- Fat: 12g

Cottage Cheese and Pineapple Cups

Ingredients:

- 1/2 cup low-fat cottage cheese

- 1/2 cup fresh pineapple chunks

Instructions:

1. Mix cottage cheese and pineapple in a bowl.

2. Serve in small cups for a refreshing snack.

Nutritional Information:

- Calories: 150

- Protein: 15g

- Carbohydrates: 20g

- Fat: 2g

Hard-boiled eggs with Avocado

Ingredients:

- 2 hard-boiled eggs

- 1/2 avocado, sliced

- Salt and pepper to taste

Instructions:

1. Slice hard-boiled eggs and avocado.

2. Sprinkle with salt and pepper.

Nutritional Information:

- Calories: 280

- Protein: 14g

- Carbohydrates: 10g

- Fat: 20g

Trail Mix

Ingredients:

- 1/4 cup almonds
- 1/4 cup walnuts
- 2 tablespoons dried cranberries
- 2 tablespoons dark chocolate chips

Instructions:

1. Mix almonds, walnuts, dried cranberries, and dark chocolate chips.
2. Portion into small snack bags for on-the-go.

Nutritional Information:

- Calories: 300
- Protein: 8g
- Carbohydrates: 20g
- Fat: 22g

Whole Grain Toast with Hummus

Ingredients:

- 2 slices whole-grain bread

- 4 tablespoons hummus

Instructions:

1. Toast whole-grain bread.

2. Spread hummus on the toasted slices.

Nutritional Information:

- Calories: 240

- Protein: 10g

- Carbohydrates: 30g

- Fat: 10g

Veggie Sticks with Guacamole

Ingredients:

- Carrot and cucumber sticks

- 1/2 cup guacamole

Instructions:

1. Slice carrots and cucumbers into sticks.

2. Dip in guacamole for a crunchy and satisfying snack.

Nutritional Information:

- Calories: 180

- Protein: 4g

- Carbohydrates: 15g

- Fat: 12g

Edamame Pods with Sea Salt

Ingredients:

- 1 cup edamame pods

- Sea salt to taste

Instructions:

1. Boil or steam edamame pods until tender.

2. Sprinkle with sea salt before enjoying.

Nutritional Information:

- Calories: 120

- Protein: 12g

- Carbohydrates: 9g

- Fat: 5g

Smoothie with Spinach and Banana

Ingredients:

- 1 cup spinach leaves

- 1 banana

- 1/2 cup Greek yogurt

- 1/2 cup almond milk

- Ice cubes

Instructions:

1. Blend spinach, banana, Greek yogurt, and almond milk until smooth.

2. Add ice cubes and blend again.

Nutritional Information:

- Calories: 200

- Protein: 15g

- Carbohydrates: 35g

- Fat: 5g

Rice Cake with Cottage Cheese and Berries

Ingredients:

- 1 rice cake

- 1/2 cup low-fat cottage cheese

- Mixed berries for topping

Instructions:

1. Spread cottage cheese on the rice cake.

2. Top with mixed berries.

Nutritional Information:

- Calories: 180

- Protein: 15g

- Carbohydrates: 25g

- Fat: 3g

Yogurt and Berry Smoothie Bowl

Ingredients:

- 1 cup plain yogurt

- 1/2 cup mixed berries

- 1 tablespoon honey

- Granola for topping

Instructions:

1. Blend yogurt and mixed berries until smooth.

2. Pour into a bowl and top with honey and granola.

Nutritional Information:

- Calories: 250

- Protein: 10g

- Carbohydrates: 40g

- Fat: 6g

Turkey Roll-Ups with Cheese

Ingredients:

- 4 slices turkey breast

- 2 slices Swiss cheese

- Mustard for dipping

Instructions:

1. Place a slice of cheese on each turkey slice.

2. Roll up and secure with toothpicks.

3. Serve with mustard for dipping.

Nutritional Information:

- Calories: 220

- Protein: 25g

- Carbohydrates: 2g

- Fat: 12g

Cucumber and Hummus Bites

Ingredients:

- Cucumber slices

- 1/4 cup hummus

- Cherry tomatoes for topping

Instructions:

1. Top cucumber slices with hummus.

2. Garnish with halved cherry tomatoes.

Nutritional Information:

- Calories: 150

- Protein: 5g

- Carbohydrates: 15g

- Fat: 8g

Almond and Berry Energy Balls

Ingredients:

- 1 cup almonds

- 1 cup dried mixed berries

- 1 tablespoon honey

- 1/2 teaspoon vanilla extract

Instructions:

1. Blend almonds and dried berries in a food processor.

2. Add honey and vanilla extract, and blend until a dough forms.

3. Roll into small energy balls.

Nutritional Information:

- Calories: 200

- Protein: 6g

- Carbohydrates: 20g

- Fat: 12g

Chapter 9

Conclusion

In conclusion, Metabolic Confusion emerges as a dynamic and adaptable approach to enhancing metabolic function specifically tailored for women. This innovative concept harnesses the principles of varying dietary and exercise patterns, strategically implementing changes to elicit a response from the body's metabolism. Throughout this exploration, we have delved into the multifaceted components that contribute to the effectiveness of Metabolic Confusion, encompassing dietary choices, workout regimens, hormonal fluctuations, and lifestyle considerations.

Metabolic Confusion for women goes beyond the conventional one-size-fits-all strategies, recognizing the inherent complexity of female physiology. The menstrual cycle, hormonal fluctuations, and unique metabolic demands are all integrated into the design of personalized and sustainable approaches. By understanding and leveraging the interplay between hormones, nutrition, and exercise, women can optimize their metabolic processes for improved energy levels, enhanced fat metabolism, and overall well-being.

The emphasis on diverse nutrient profiles, including a mix of macronutrients and micronutrients, fosters a balanced and nourishing diet. This not only supports metabolic flexibility but also addresses the specific nutritional needs of women, especially during different phases of the menstrual cycle. The inclusion of whole foods, lean proteins, healthy fats, and a variety of colorful fruits and vegetables ensures that the body receives the essential building blocks for optimal metabolic function.

In the realm of physical activity, the incorporation of diverse workout modalities such as strength training, high-intensity intervals, and cardiovascular exercises introduces a layer of unpredictability that challenges the body in novel ways. This variety prevents the development of plateaus and keeps the metabolism responsive to different stimuli, thereby promoting continuous improvement in fitness levels, muscle tone, and overall metabolic health.

Furthermore, recognizing the importance of recovery, stress management, and quality sleep within the Metabolic Confusion framework is crucial. These lifestyle factors play pivotal roles in hormonal balance and overall metabolic efficiency. The interconnectedness of stress, cortisol levels, and metabolic health underscores the need for holistic well-being strategies that extend beyond diet and exercise alone.

As we navigate the intricacies of Metabolic Confusion for women, it is evident that this approach empowers individuals to embrace the uniqueness of their bodies. By tailoring strategies to align with the ebb and flow of hormonal cycles, women can optimize metabolic outcomes, fostering sustainable health improvements. However, it is essential to approach Metabolic Confusion with mindfulness, listening to the body's cues and adjusting strategies accordingly.

In essence, Metabolic Confusion for women is not a rigid set of rules but a guiding principle that encourages flexibility, adaptation, and a holistic approach to health. As we move forward, further research and exploration will likely unveil additional nuances and refinements to this concept, enhancing its applicability and efficacy in promoting metabolic health for women across diverse backgrounds and lifestyles. Through ongoing collaboration between health professionals, researchers, and individuals, Metabolic Confusion stands as an exciting frontier in the pursuit of personalized and sustainable approaches to women's metabolic well-being.

www.ingramcontent.com/pod-product-compliance
Lightning Source LLC
Chambersburg PA
CBHW071605270726
48661CB00018B/1410